WAR PLANES

High-Altitude Spy Planes:
The U-2s

by Bill Sweetman

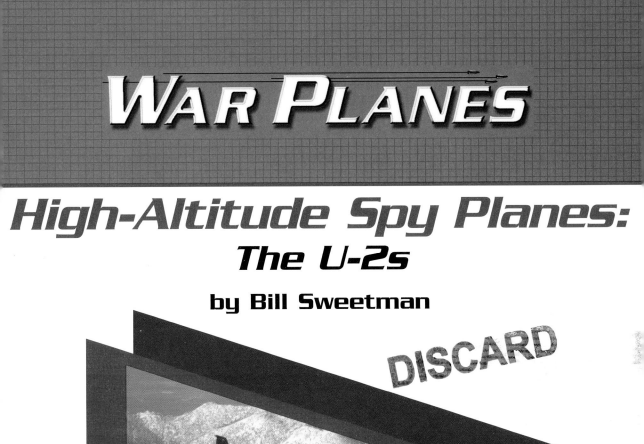

DISCARD

CAPSTONE
HIGH-INTEREST
BOOKS

an imprint of Capstone Press
Mankato, Minnesota

Capstone High-Interest Books are published by Capstone Press
151 Good Counsel Drive, P.O. Box 669, Mankato, Minnesota 56002
http://www.capstone-press.com

Library of Congress Cataloging-in-Publication Data
Sweetman, Bill.
    High-altitude spy planes: the U-2s / by Bill Sweetman.
    p. cm.—(War Planes)
    Includes bibliographical references and index.
    ISBN 0-7368-0790-X
    1. U-2 (Reconnaissance aircraft)—Juvenile literature. [1. U-2
(Reconnaissance aircraft) 2. Airplanes, Military] I. Title. II. War Planes
(Mankato, Minn.)
UG1242.R4 S9423 2001
623.7'467—dc21   00-010400

Summary: Discusses the U-2 spy plane, its uses, engines, sensors, and future in
the U.S. Air Force.

Editorial Credits
Matt Doeden, editor; Lois Wallentine, product planning editor; Timothy
    Halldin, cover designer and illustrator; Katy Kudela, photo researcher

Photo Credits
AFFTC History Office, 1, 10, 24
Defense Visual Information Center, 28
Eric Schulzinger/Lockheed Martin Corp., cover
Ted Carlson/Fotodynamics, 4, 6, 9, 13, 16–17, 18, 20, 23, 27

**Special thanks to the U.S. Air Force Air Combat Command for their help in
preparing this book.**

1 2 3 4 5 6 06 05 04 03 02 01

Table of Contents

Chapter One

Learn About

- The U-2's mission
- Military intelligence
- Early U-2 flights

The U-2 in Action

It is a rainy night in eastern Europe. A group of soldiers is moving tanks and weapons toward the border of a neighboring country. The soldiers are preparing for a surprise invasion.

A black U-2 spy plane flies slowly in a wide circle 70 miles (113 kilometers) away. The plane is 12 miles (19 kilometers) above the ground. The soldiers below do not know that the U-2 is taking photographs of everything that they do.

The U-2 is designed to gather military intelligence.

Three U.S. Air Force officers watch a computer screen on the other side of the world. They are located at Beale Air Force Base in California. One of the U-2's photographs of the enemy soldiers appears on the screen. The officers realize that the enemy is planning an attack.

The Air Force officers send the photograph to their leaders in Washington, D.C. Within hours, U.S. military forces in Europe are ready to defend against the attack.

Building the U-2

Military intelligence is information about an enemy's plans and actions. Intelligence is important to military leaders. They use it to prepare for battles and to avoid battles. In the 1950s, U.S. military leaders wanted to build a spy plane to gather information about enemies. This action is called reconnaissance.

The U.S. military wanted a plane that could fly very high. It also wanted a plane that could fly long distances without stopping for fuel. Military leaders asked an aircraft builder called the Lockheed Aircraft Corporation to build such a plane. The code name for this plane was U-2.

Lockheed designed and built the U-2 in secret. The company tested the U-2 on a secret base in Nevada. The Air Force still uses this base to test aircraft. The base sometimes is called Area 51.

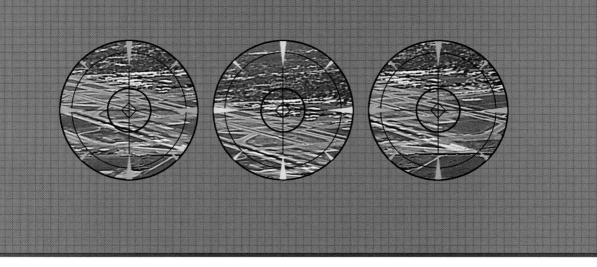

About the U-2

In 1956, the U-2 made its first reconnaissance flight over the Soviet Union. Today, the area that was the Soviet Union is split into Russia and several smaller countries. The U.S. military thought that there might be a war someday with the Soviet Union. U.S. military officials wanted to know everything they could about the Soviet military.

In 1960, the Soviet Union's military shot down a U-2. Soviet officials captured the plane's pilot. His name was Francis Gary Powers. Powers later admitted that he had been spying on the Soviet Union. The Soviet government sentenced Powers to 10 years in prison. But the Soviet Union released him after just two years.

Pilots call the U-2 the Dragon Lady.

The U.S. military stopped flying U-2s over the Soviet Union after 1960. But it continued to use the plane elsewhere. In the 1960s, Lockheed built a bigger version of the U-2. It was called the U-2R.

The U-2 still is important for gathering intelligence today. The U.S. Air Force has about 40 U-2s. The U-2 has no official Air Force nickname. Its pilots sometimes call it the Dragon Lady after a spy in an old comic strip.

Chapter Two

Learn About

- U-2 specifications
- Body design
- Engine

Inside the U-2

The U-2 does not look like any other U.S. military airplane. The U-2's wingspan measures 103 feet (31 meters). Wingspan is the distance between the tips of the wings. Most military planes have a short wingspan. But the U-2's wingspan is as long as the wingspans of some jet airliners.

The U-2 also is lightweight. It is lighter than some fighter planes. The U-2 weighs only about 11,700 pounds (5,300 kilograms) when empty.

Body Design

Lockheed designed the U-2 to be simple, dependable, and lightweight. The wings and body are made of a lightweight metal called aluminum. Tanks in the wings hold up to 9 tons (8 metric tons) of fuel.

The U-2's body is designed to allow it to reach high altitudes. Altitude is the measure of an object's height above the ground. The U-2's wings are long and straight. This gives the plane the highest possible lift.

The U-2's long wings allow it to fly as high as 80,000 feet (24,400 meters). This distance is about 15 miles (24 kilometers) above the ground. Flying at this altitude helps keep the U-2 safe from many enemy weapons. It also puts pilots in a good position to take photographs of the land below.

The plane's fuselage is long and narrow. A fuselage is the main body of a plane. The narrow fuselage gives the plane a low amount of air resistance. This force of air slows down moving objects.

Designers built special landing gear for the U-2. Normal landing gear for a plane of the U-2's size is heavy. Heavy landing gear would prevent U-2 pilots from flying as high as necessary. Most of the U-2's weight is carried on a single two-wheeled landing leg. A small tailwheel helps to steer the plane on the ground. This small landing gear makes landing difficult for pilots.

The U-2 has special lightweight landing gear.

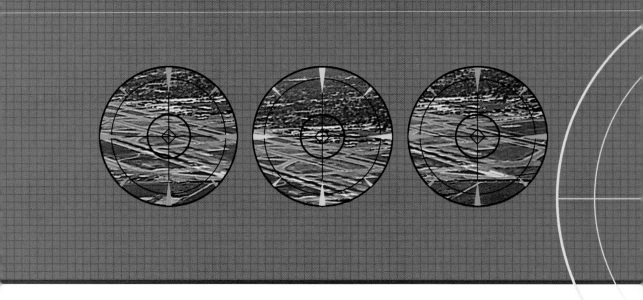

Engine

The U-2 is powered by a single jet engine. This engine produces about 17,000 pounds (7,700 kilograms) of thrust. The engine's thrust pushes the airplane forward through the air.

A U-2 pilot pulls the plane into a steep climb after takeoff. The jet engine pushes the plane to its cruising altitude of 80,000 feet (24,400 meters). This climb may take less than 30 minutes. Pilots usually fly U-2s at about 460 miles (740 kilometers) per hour once they reach cruising altitude.

A U-2 pilot must take care to keep the plane's engine running at high altitudes. The air at the U-2's cruising altitude contains very little

U-2 Specifications

Function:	High-altitude reconnaissance
Manufacturer:	Lockheed Aircraft Corporation
Date Deployed:	1955
Length:	63 feet (19.2 meters)
Wingspan:	103 feet (31 meters)
Height:	16 feet (4.9 meters)
Weight:	11,700 pounds (5,300 kilograms)
Payload:	3,000 pounds (1,360 kilograms)
Engine:	One Pratt and Whitney J75-P-13B or one General Electric F110-GE-100/129
Thrust:	17,000 pounds (7,700 kilograms)
Top Speed:	475 miles (765 kilometers) per hour
Ceiling:	80,000 feet (24,400 meters)
Range:	7,000 miles (11,300 kilometers)

oxygen. Jet engines need oxygen to burn fuel. Jet engines that do not receive enough oxygen stall. Stalled engines are difficult to restart at high altitudes. A U-2 pilot must keep the plane's speed high to force enough oxygen into the engine.

tail

fuel tank

tail wheel

The U-2

wing

cockpit

nose

landing gear

Chapter Three

Learn About

- Spy equipment
- Payload
- Pressure suits

Sensors and Tactics

U-2 pilots use a variety of sensors and scientific equipment to perform their missions. Sensors record information about what is happening on the ground below. U-2s may carry cameras, radar, radio antennas, and scientific equipment. Pilots use these sensors and equipment to gather information about an area.

U-2 pilots take photographs from high altitudes.

Sensors

The U-2 does not carry guns and missiles like most military planes. It carries sensors instead. U.S. military officials depend on information from U-2 sensors to learn about the enemy.

Cameras are the most important sensors for U-2 reconnaissance. In the 1950s and 1960s, U-2 pilots flew directly over targets to take photos. But today, U-2s have much more powerful cameras. Pilots can take photos of targets from as far as 100 miles (160 kilometers) away. Enemies rarely detect U-2s from this distance.

U-2s also carry many electronic sensors. These sensors include radar equipment and radio antennas. Radar equipment uses radio waves to locate objects. Pilots use radar to create detailed maps of an area. They use the antennas to pick up enemy radio signals.

U-2s sometimes carry as much as 3,000 pounds (1,360 kilograms) of sensor equipment. The total weight of the equipment a U-2 carries is called the payload. Most sensors are located along the plane's long nose or under the wings. Some are located in an area behind the cockpit.

Adaptability

The sensors a U-2 carries depend on its mission. U-2s carry only the equipment they need. Sensors on a U-2 can be replaced and changed easily. This keeps the plane's weight low.

Each mission requires different equipment. For example, a night mission may require a radar device connected to powerful computers. The computers can make maps based on the information the radar device collects. A day mission may require a camera with a telescopic lens. This special lens makes distant objects appear closer. The lens allows pilots to take detailed photographs from a great distance.

Other Equipment

The air at 80,000 feet (24,400 meters) does not contain enough oxygen for people to breathe. The U-2's cockpit must be pressurized for pilots to survive. Machines pump air into the cockpit to keep air pressure high. But this is not enough. The cockpit cannot be pressurized if the U-2's engine stops. The pilot might become unconscious before the engine could be restarted.

U-2 pilots wear pressure suits.

U-2 pilots must wear pressure suits to protect themselves from this danger. The suit covers the pilot's entire body. A pressure suit includes a helmet, a sealed visor, and heavy gloves. The suit provides air pressure to a pilot's entire body. A pilot wearing a pressure suit can survive even if a U-2's engine stops. The pilot then has time to restart the engine.

Pilots may spend many hours on a mission. They must keep their energy high. Pilots carry small tubes of high-energy food with them. The tubes look like toothpaste tubes.

Chapter Four

Learn About

Changes to the U-2
Additional U-2 uses
Future plans

The Future

The U.S. Air Force has been using U-2s for more than 40 years. Today, it has about 40 U-2s in service. Technology has changed a great deal since the U-2 was first used in the 1950s. The Air Force works to keep the U-2 up to date. Updated communication devices and sensors have kept the airplane useful through the years.

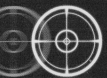

Updates

The Air Force is making several changes to keep the U-2 modern. The pilot controls inside the U-2's cockpit are made up of dials and switches. Few modern airplanes include this kind of control system. The Air Force is changing the U-2's controls. It is replacing the dials and switches with computer controls.

The Air Force also is updating the U-2's sensors. Military leaders want immediate access to intelligence. Some U-2s now carry a satellite antenna. This device allows pilots to send information to a satellite orbiting Earth. The satellite then can instantly send the information anywhere on Earth.

New sensors also are making the U-2 more effective. Some new sensors are combinations of two or more old sensors. For example, one

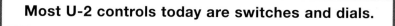

Most U-2 controls today are switches and dials.

new sensor combines radar information with infra-red information. Infra-red sensors detect heat. The combination of radar and infra-red sensors can create pictures of objects inside thick forests.

U-2s sometimes are used for scientific research.

The U-2's Future

Today, the U-2 remains one of the U.S. military's most important reconnaissance tools. U-2s have provided intelligence in recent conflicts such as the Gulf War (1991).

U-2s are used for more than just reconnaissance. Scientists sometimes use the planes for scientific research. Scientists send equipment up with some U-2s to take measurements of Earth's atmosphere. U-2s have gathered information that has helped scientists learn about the Earth's ozone layer. U-2 photos also have helped scientists study the effects of volcanic eruptions.

Some military leaders want to build more U-2s. They believe current U-2 ground crews and pilots are overworked. That is because no other U.S. military plane can do what the U-2 does. For this reason, the U-2 will remain important to the U.S. military for many years to come.

Words to Know

aluminum (uh-LOO-mi-nuhm)—a lightweight, silver-colored metal; most airplanes are made of aluminum.

antenna (an-TEN-uh)—a wire or dish that sends or receives radio waves

fuselage (FYOO-suh-lahzh)—the main body of an airplane

intelligence (in-TEL-uh-jenss)—knowledge about an enemy's plans and actions

mission (MISH-uhn)—a military task

payload (PAY-lohd)—the total weight of the equipment carried by a U-2

pressurize (PRESH-uh-rize)—to seal off an airplane cockpit so that the air pressure is the same as at the Earth's surface

radar (RAY-dar)—equipment that uses radio waves to locate and guide objects

reconnaissance mission (ree-KON-uh-suhnss MISH-uhn)—a mission to gather information about an enemy

thrust (THRUHST)—the force created by a jet engine; thrust pushes an airplane forward.

To Learn More

Green, Michael. *The United States Air Force.* Serving Your Country. Mankato, Minn.: Capstone High-Interest Books, 1998.

Maynard, Christopher. *Aircraft.* The Need for Speed. Minneapolis: Lerner Publications, 1999.

Schleifer, Jay. *Spy Planes.* Wings. Mankato, Minn.: Capstone Books, 1996.

Useful Addresses

Air Combat Command
Office of Public Affairs
115 Thompson Street, Suite 211
Langley Air Force Base, VA 23665

Air Force History Support Office
Reference and Analysis Division
200 McChord Street, Box 94
Bolling AFB, DC 20332

Internet Sites

FAS Intelligence Resource Program–The U-2

http://www.fas.org/irp/program/collect/u-2.htm

Smithsonian National Air and Space Museum

http://www.nasm.edu

The United States Air Force

http://www.af.mil

Index